Everybody's Pickin' on Leiber & Stoller

T0061285

Music transcriptions by Paul Pappas and David Stocker

ISBN 978-1-4584-1849-4

HAL•LEONARD®
CORPORATION

7777 W. BLUEMOUND RD. P.O. BOX 13819 MILWAUKEE, WI 53213

Visit Hal Leonard Online at
www.halleonard.com

Stand by Me

Words and Music by Jerry Leiber, Mike Stoller and Ben E. King
Arranged by Nick Charles

*Drop D tuning, partial Capo II:
(low to high) D-A-D-G-B-E

*Tune guitar as indicated and place capo at 2nd fret so that it covers all but the 1st string.
Capoed fret is "0" and open 1st string is "-2" in tab.

**Chord symbols in parentheses represent chord names respective to capoed guitar.
Symbols above represent actual sounding chords. Chord symbols reflect implied harmony.

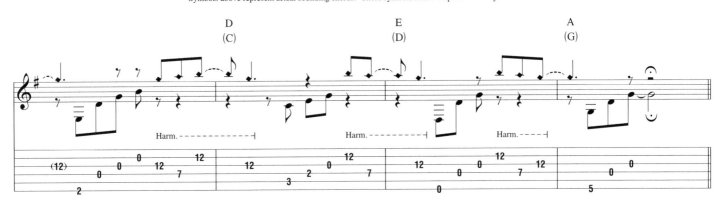

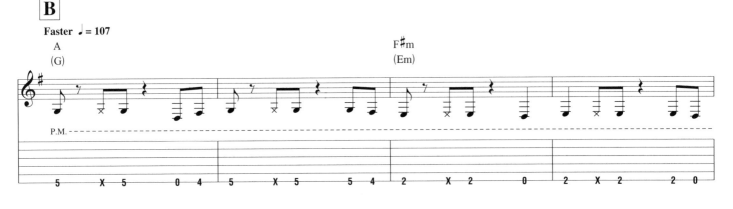

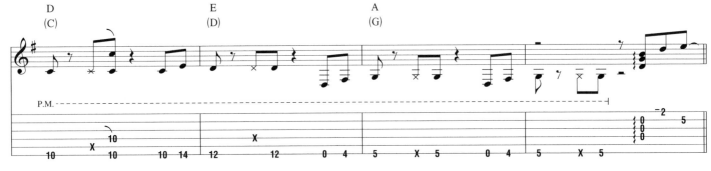

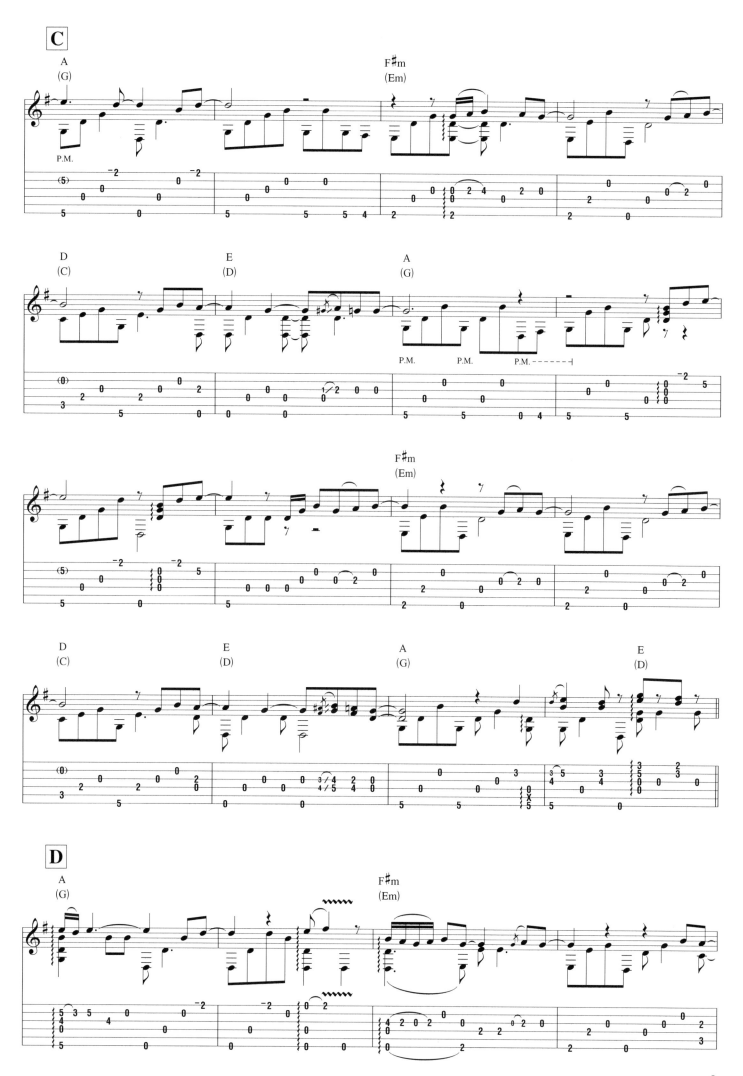

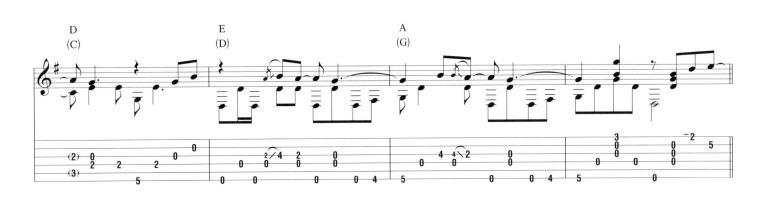

E

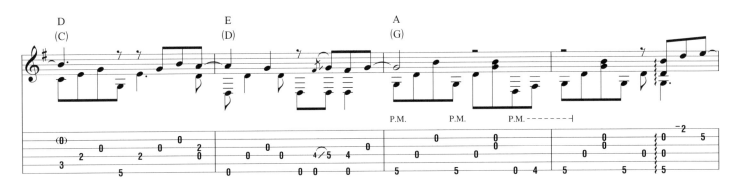

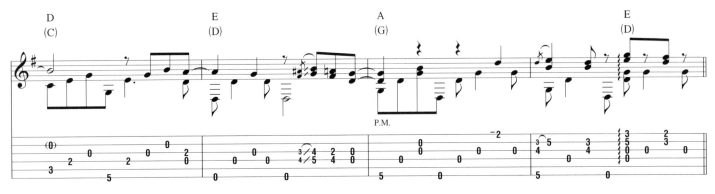

Kansas City

Words and Music by Jerry Leiber and Mike Stoller
Arranged by Mark Hanson

Open G7 tuning, down 1/2 step:
(low to high) C#-F#-E-F#-A#-C#

*Chord symbols reflect implied harmony.

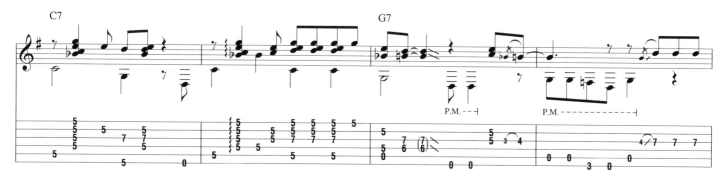

C

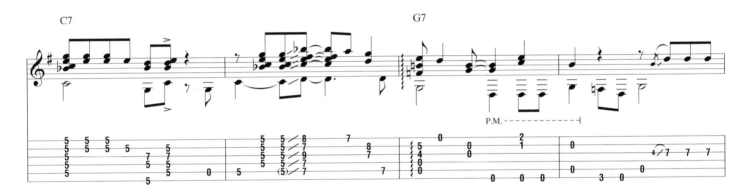

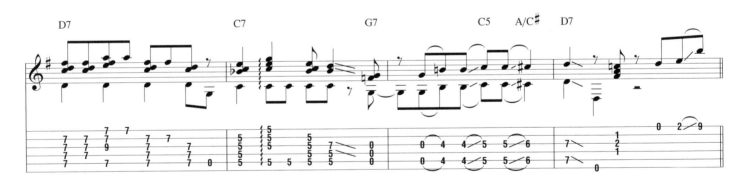

D

F

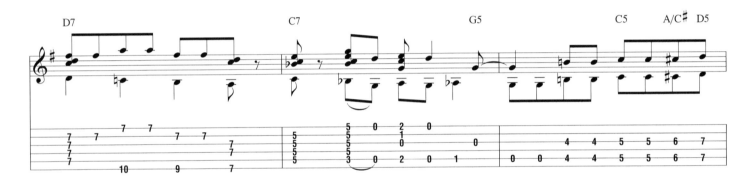

G

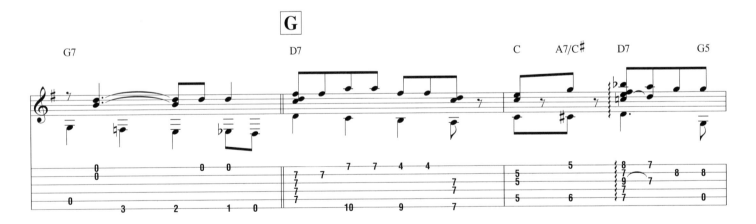

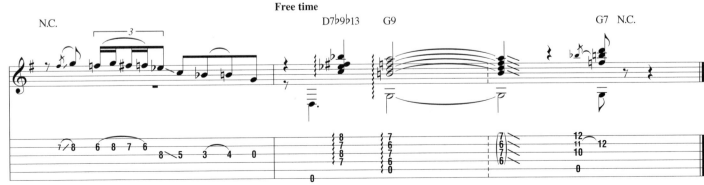

Charlie Brown

Words and Music by Jerry Leiber and Mike Stoller
Arranged by Arlen Roth

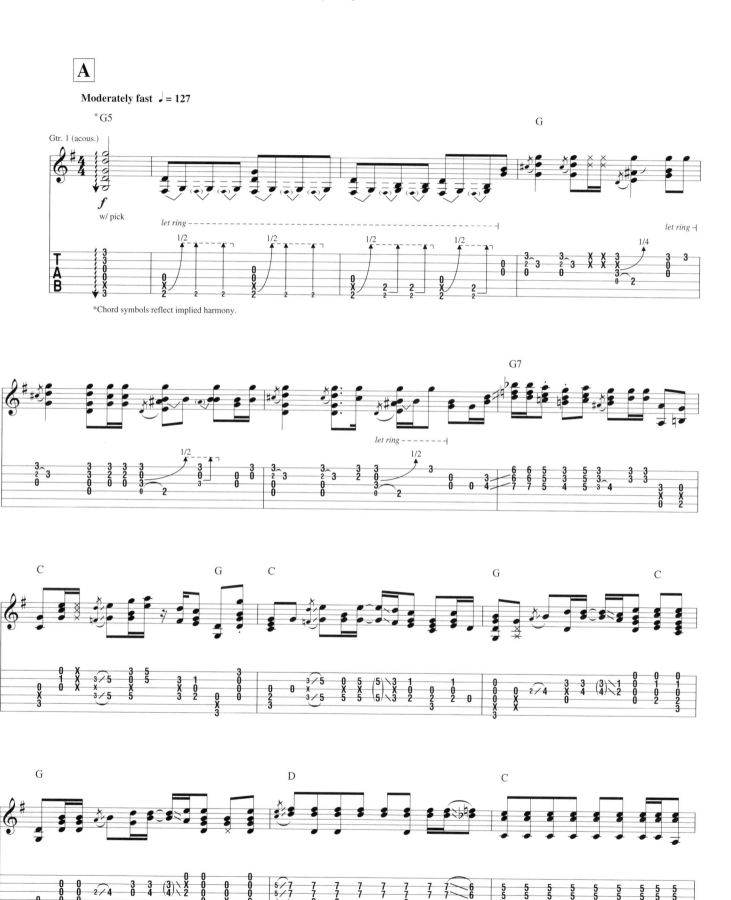

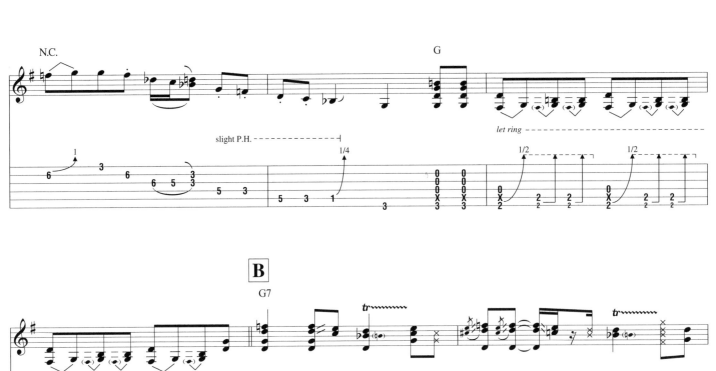

B

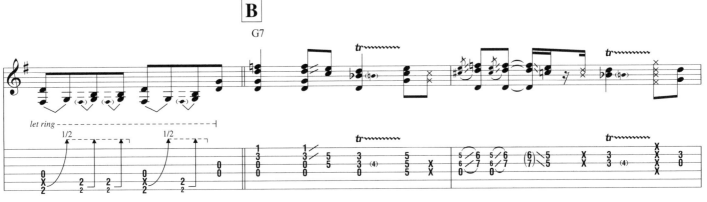

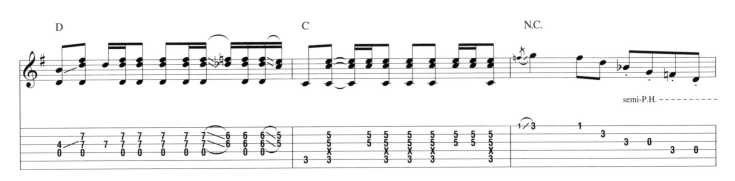

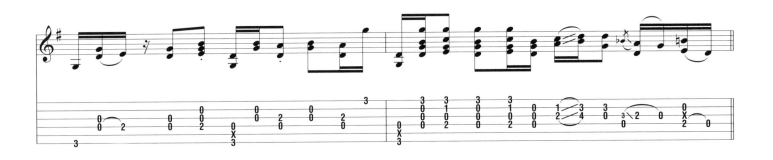

E

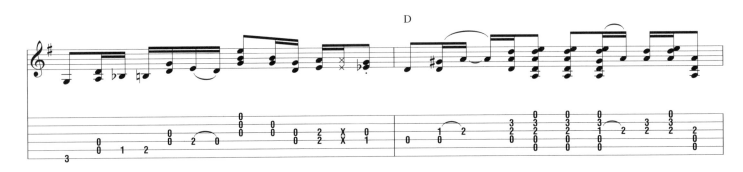

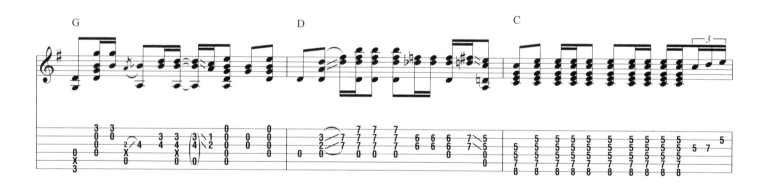

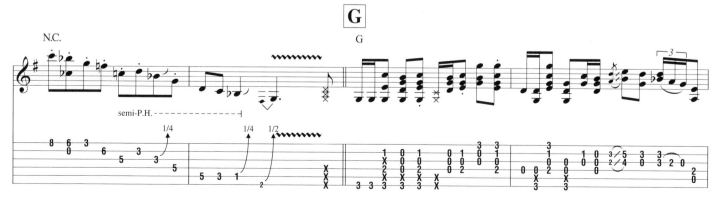

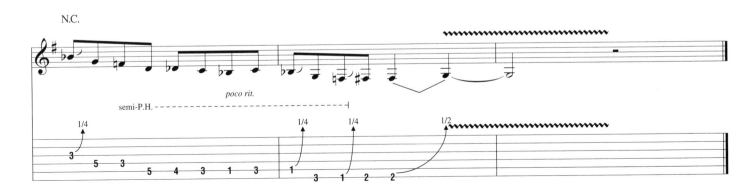

Fools Fall in Love

Words and Music by Jerry Leiber and Mike Stoller
Arranged by Doug Smith

Drop D tuning:
(low to high) D-A-D-G-B-E

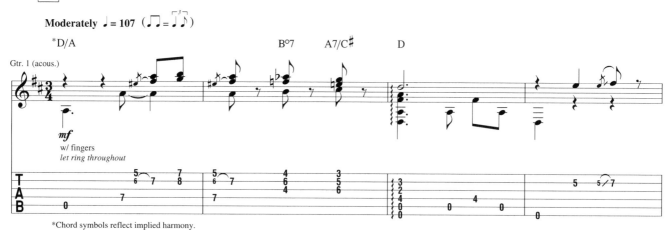

*Chord symbols reflect implied harmony.

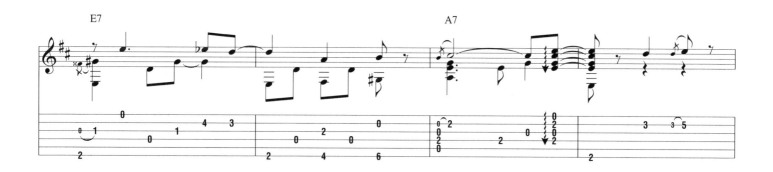

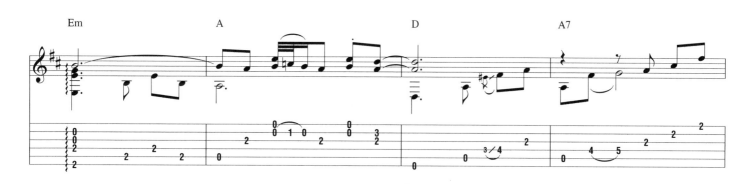

B

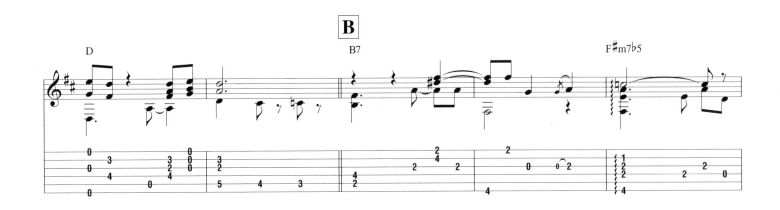

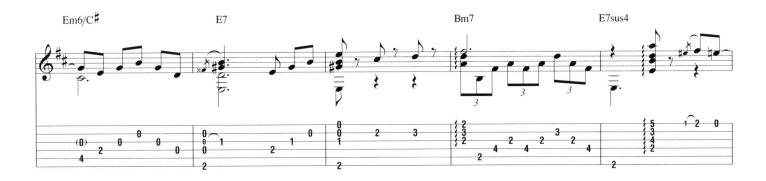

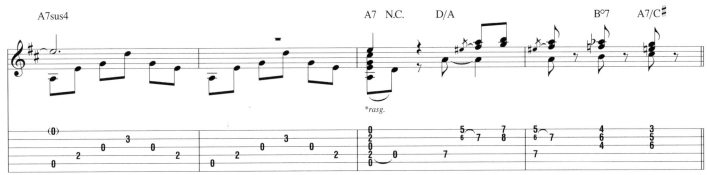

*Rasgueado: Strum using backs of pick-hand fingers.

C

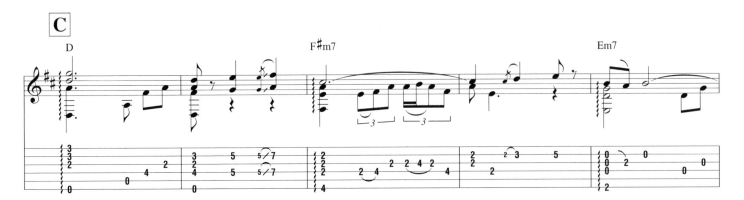

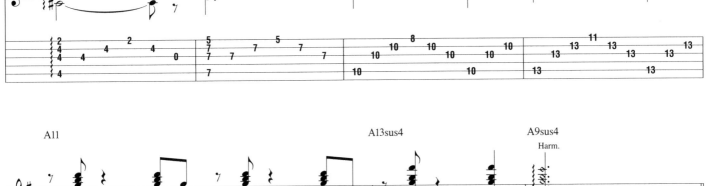

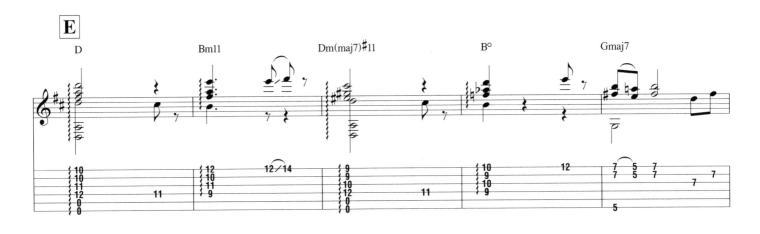

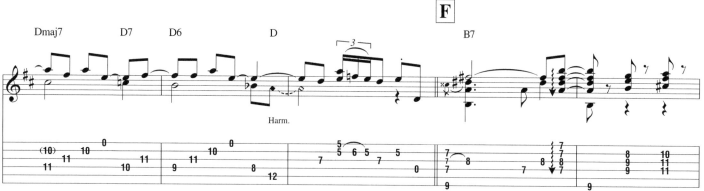

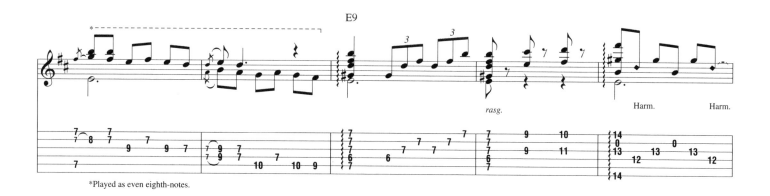

*Played as even eighth-notes.

On Broadway

Words and Music by Barry Mann, Cynthia Weil, Mike Stoller and Jerry Leiber
Arranged by David Cullen

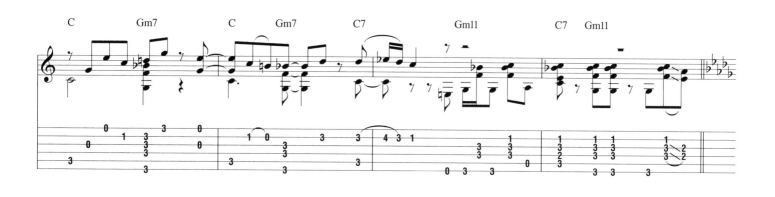

B

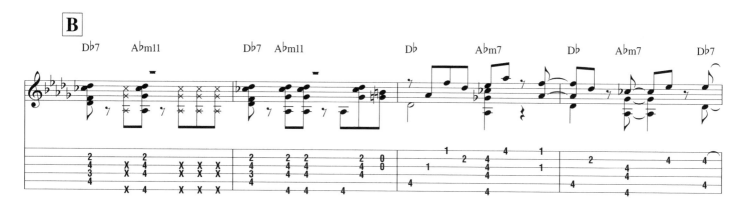

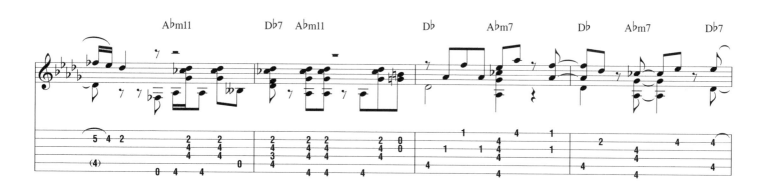

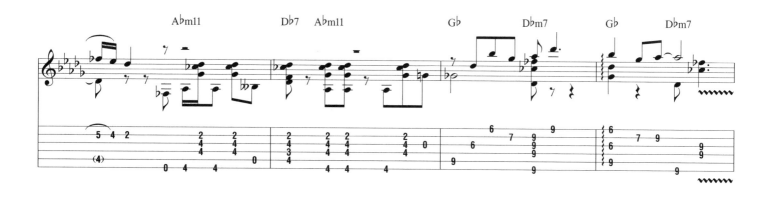

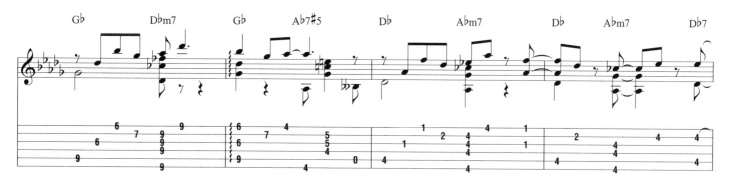

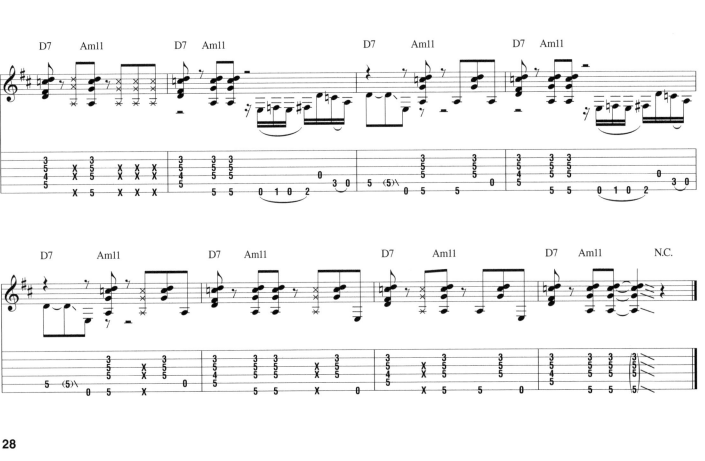

Love Me

Words and Music by Jerry Leiber and Mike Stoller
Arranged by Elliot Easton

*Two gtrs. arr. for one.
**See top of page for chord diagrams pertaining to rhythm slashes.

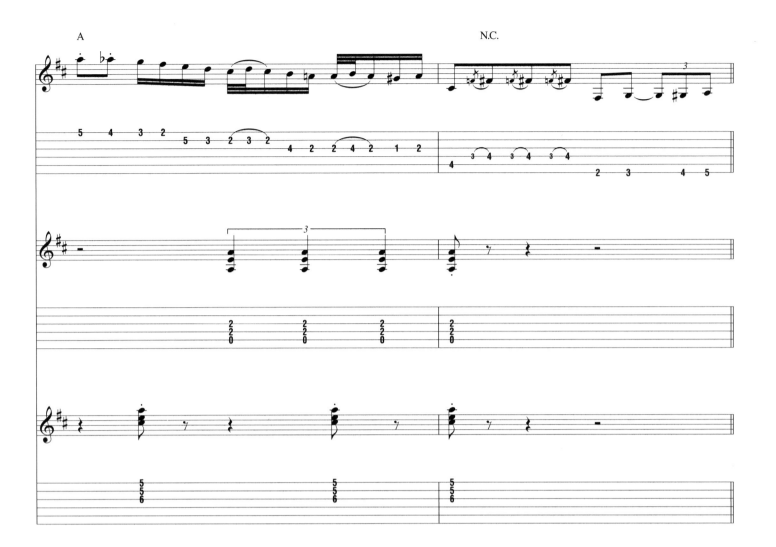

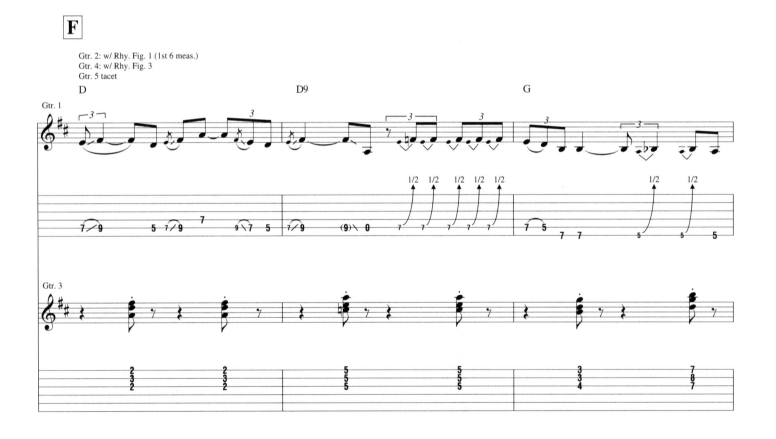

Poison Ivy

Words and Music by Jerry Leiber and Mike Stoller
Arranged by Laurence Juber

DADGAD tuning:
(low to high) D-A-D-G-A-D

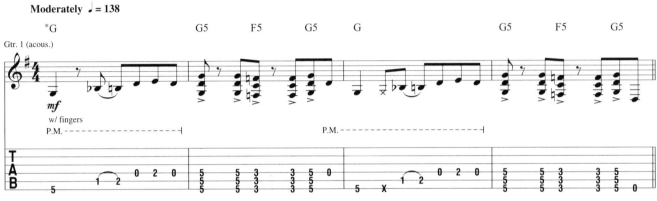

*Chord symbols reflect implied harmony.

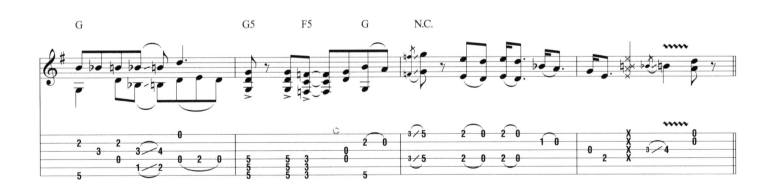

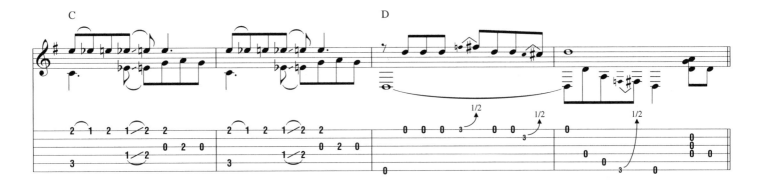

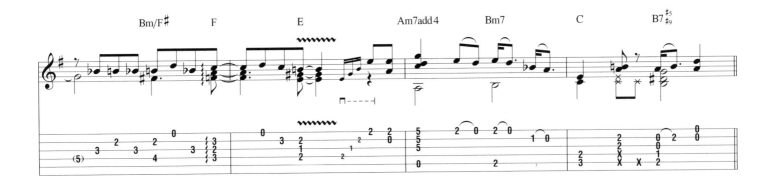

K

D.W. Washburn

Words and Music by Jerry Leiber and Mike Stoller
Arranged by Mike Dowling

Tune down 1 step:
(low to high) D-G-C-F-A-D

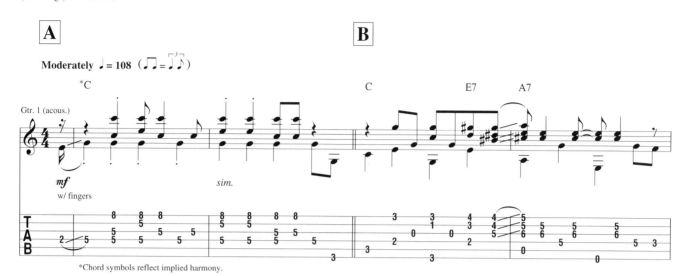

*Chord symbols reflect implied harmony.

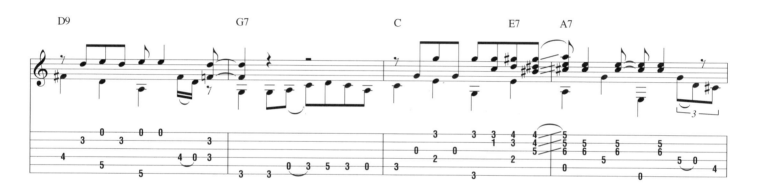

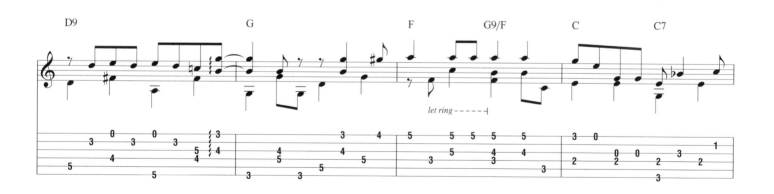

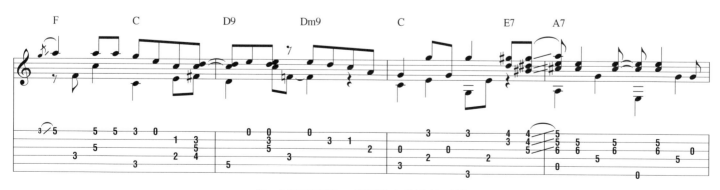

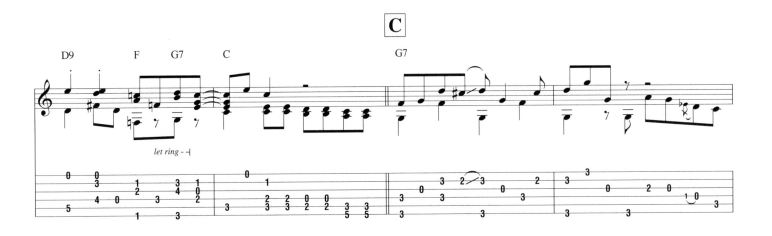

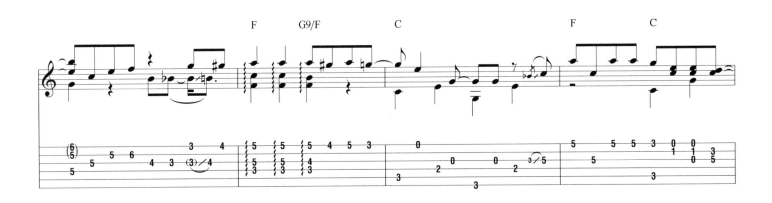

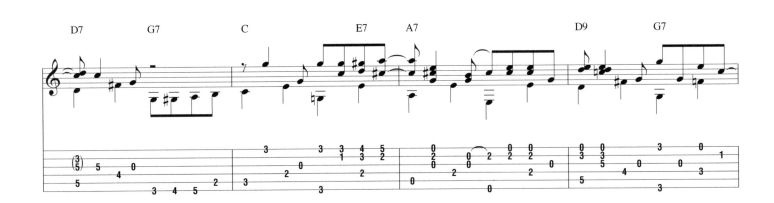

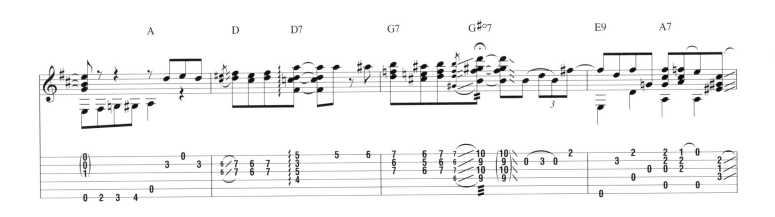

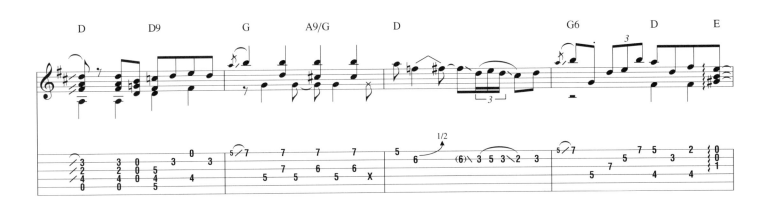

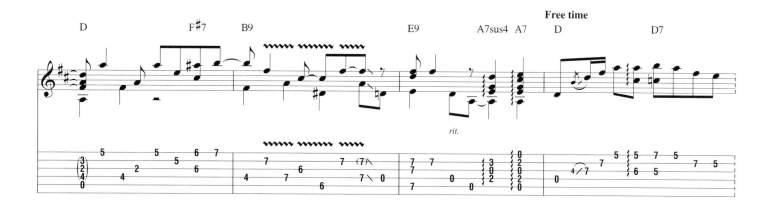

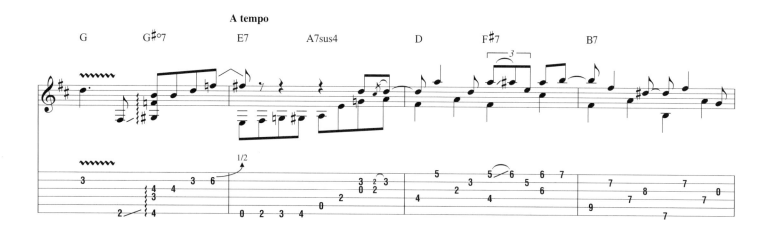

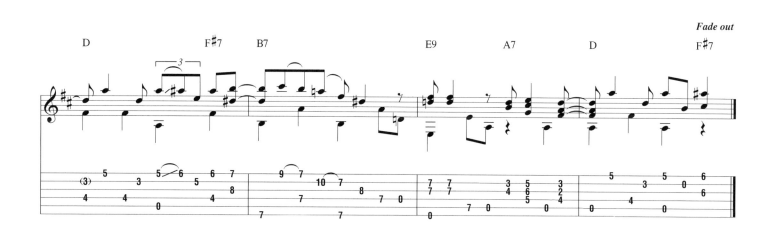

Bossa Nova Baby

Words and Music by Jerry Leiber and Mike Stoller
Arranged by Greg Hawkes

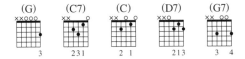

*Ukulele arr. for gtr.

**Ukulele arr. for gtr.

***Ukulele arr. for gtr.
†Two ukuleles arr. for one gtr.
††Symbols in parentheses represent chord names respective to capoed guitars and do not reflect actual sounding chords.
Capoed fret is "0" in tab. See top of page for chord diagrams pertaining to rhythm slashes.

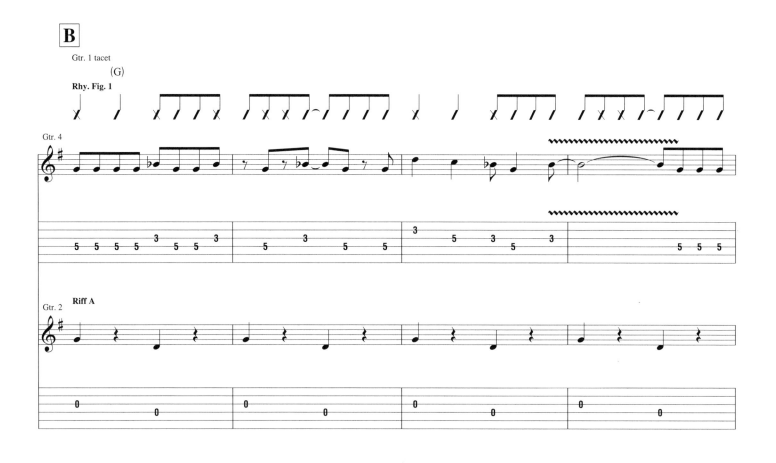

End Rhy. Fig. 1

End Riff A

Gtr. 2: w/ Riff A
Gtr. 3: w/ Rhy. Fig. 1

*Symbols in parentheses represent chord names respective to capoed guitars.
Symbols above reflect actual sounding chords.

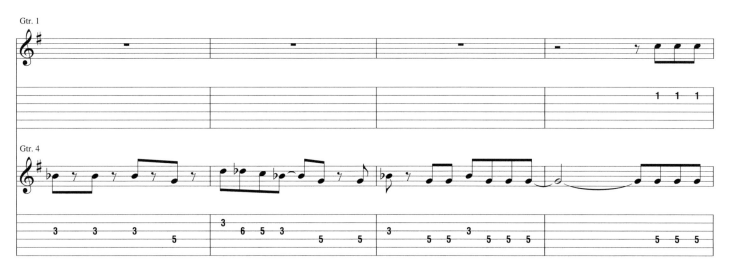

54

G

Gtr. 2: w/ Riff A
Gtr. 3: w/ Rhy. Fig. 1
Gtr. 5 tacet

Searchin'

Words and Music by Jerry Leiber and Mike Stoller
Arranged by Alex de Grassi

DADGAD tuning:
(low to high) D-A-D-G-A-D

Moderately fast ♩ = 76

*Chord symbols reflect implied harmony.

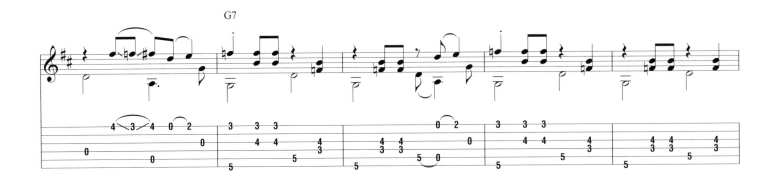

G7

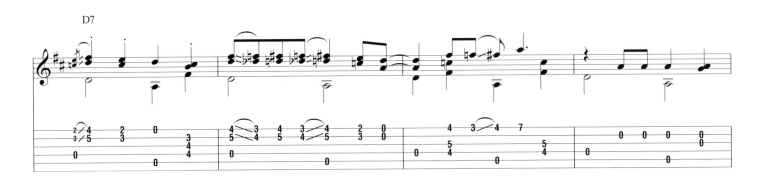

D7

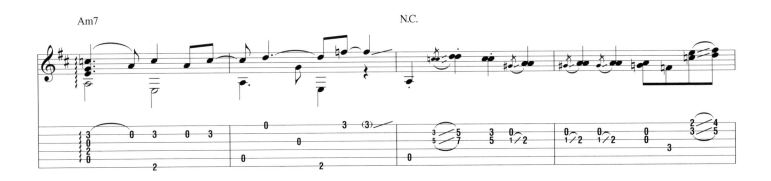

Am7   N.C.

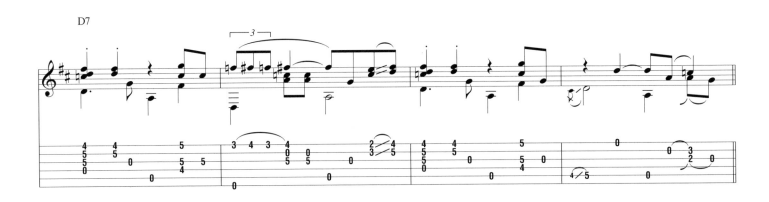

D7

C

D7

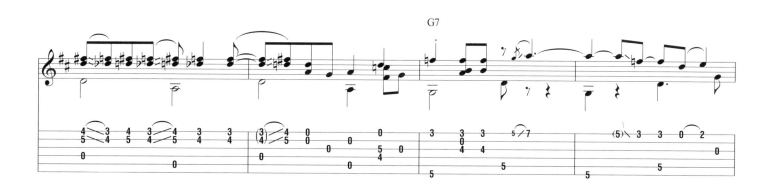

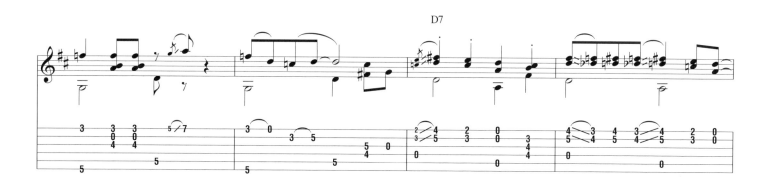

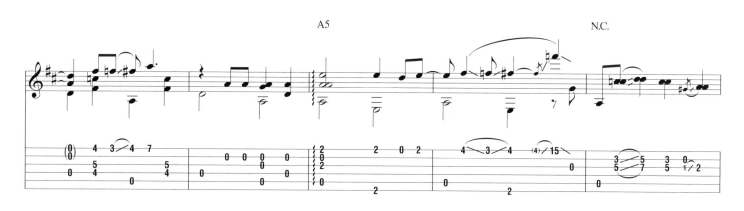

D

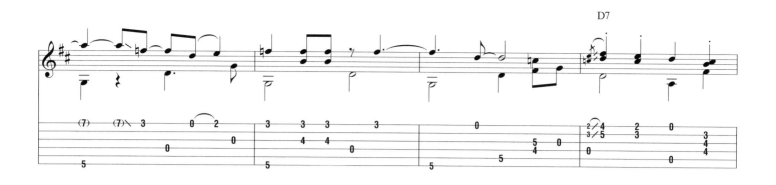

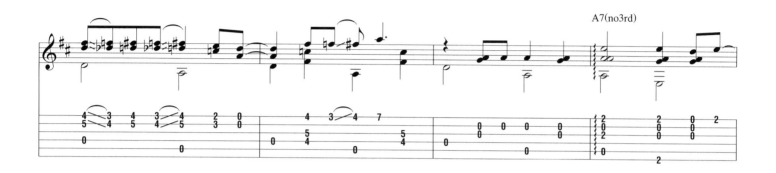

Fade out

Jailhouse Rock

Words and Music by Jerry Leiber and Mike Stoller
Arranged by Eltjo Haselhoff

Open G tuning:
(low to high) D-G-D-G-B-D

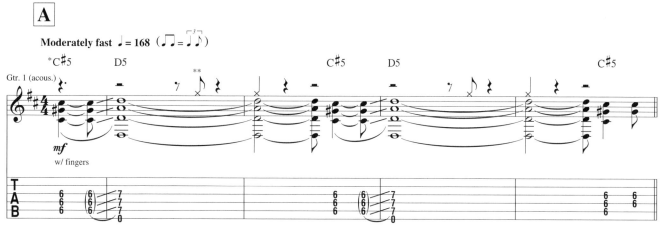

*Chord symbols reflect basic harmony.   **Tap face of guitar with right hand in rhythm indicated.

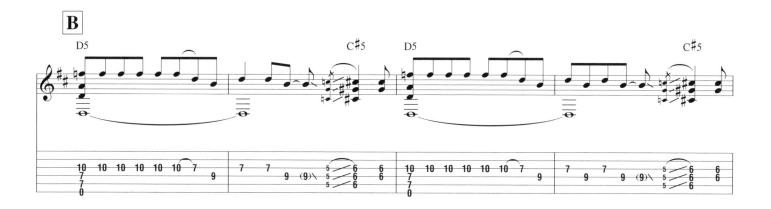

***P.M. refers to downstem
notes throughout, unless
otherwise indicated.

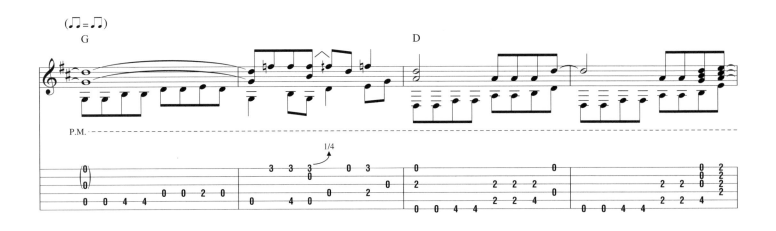

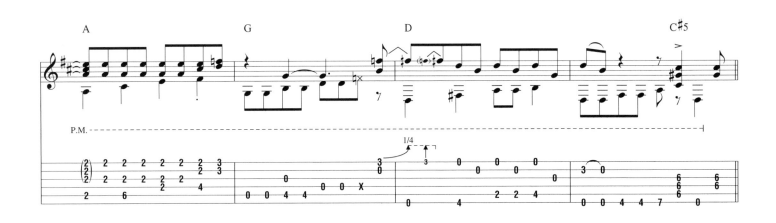

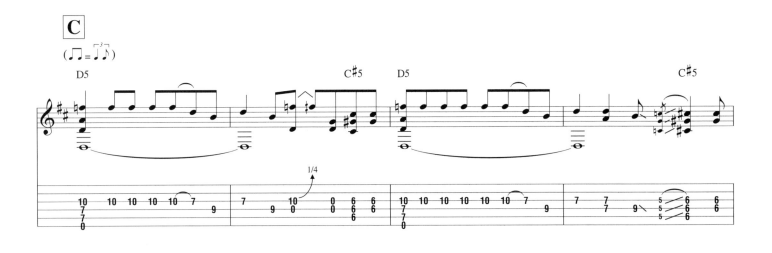

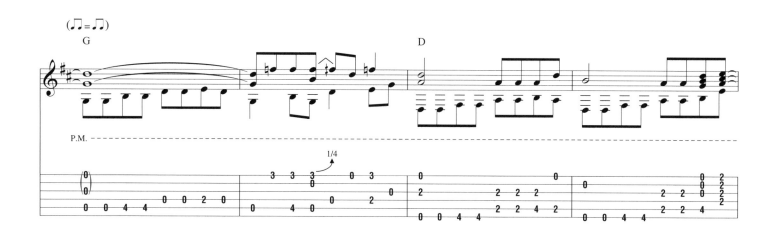

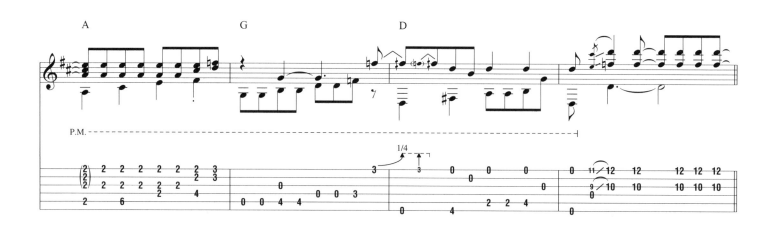

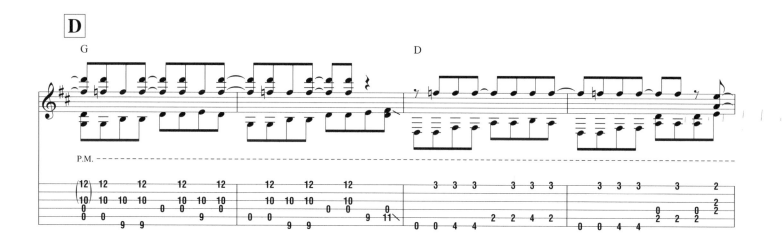

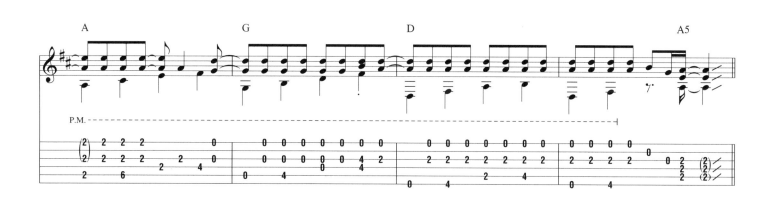

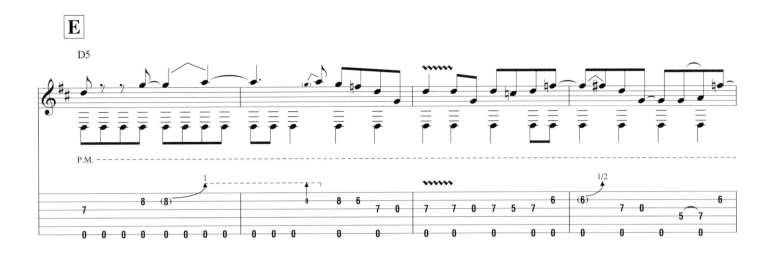

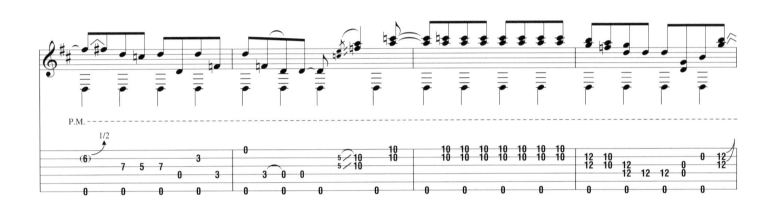

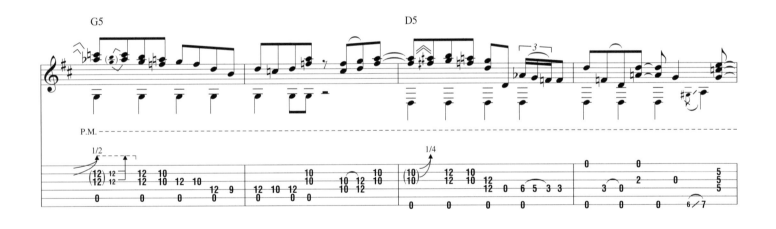

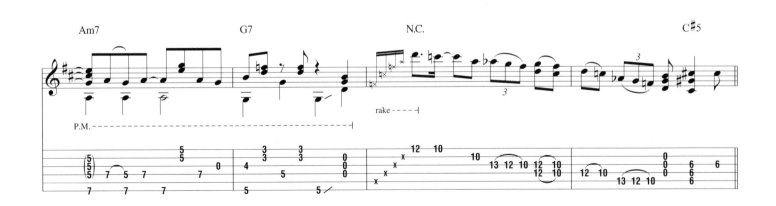

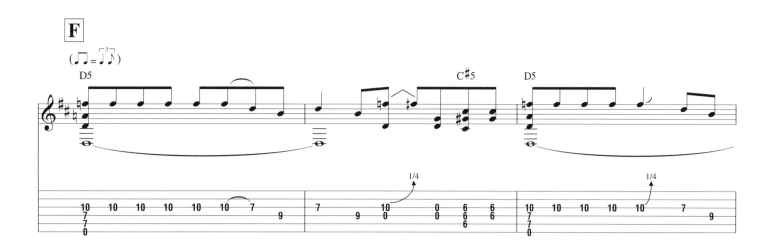

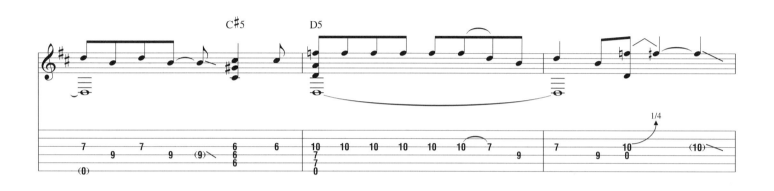

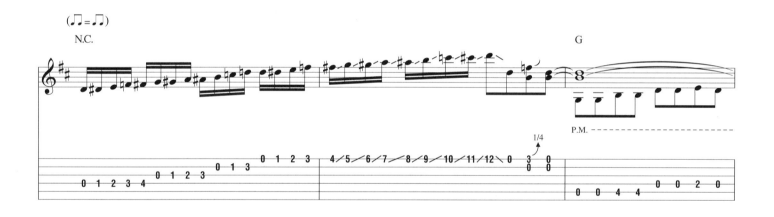

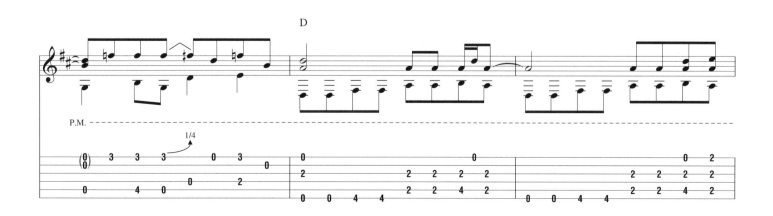

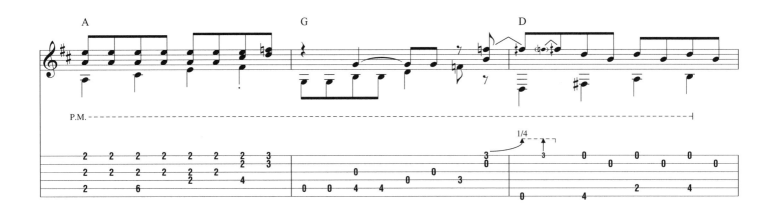

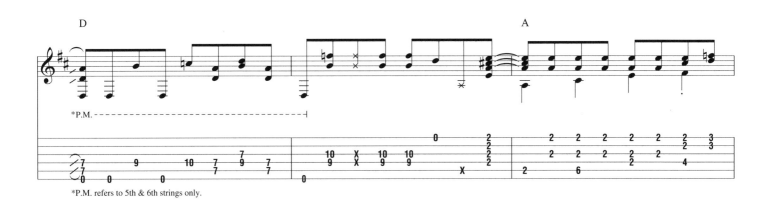

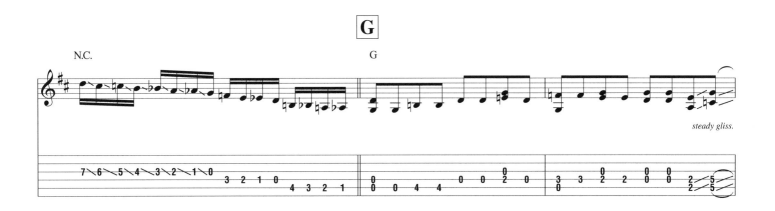

*P.M. refers to 5th & 6th strings only.

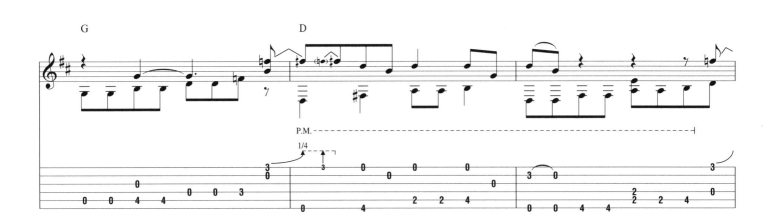

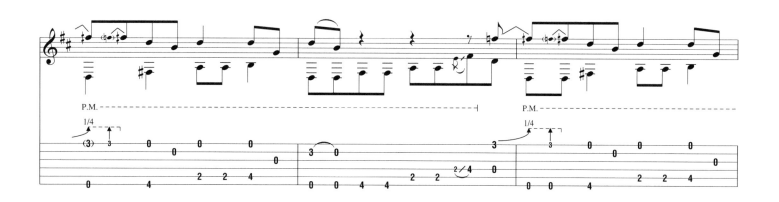

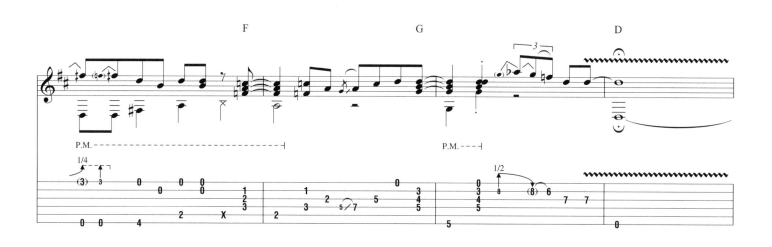

Free time

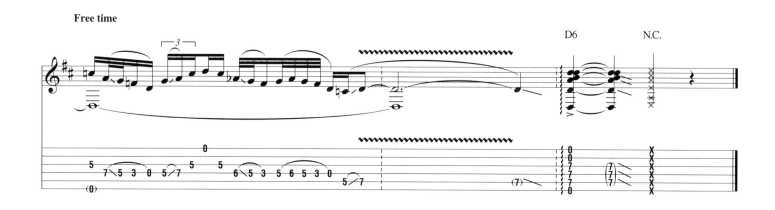

Love Potion Number 9

Words and Music by Jerry Leiber and Mike Stoller
Arranged by Al Petteway

DADGAD tuning:
(low to high) D-A-D-G-A-D

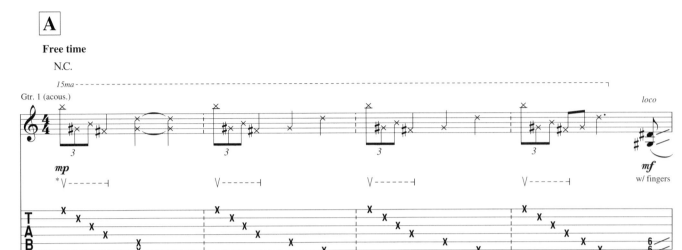

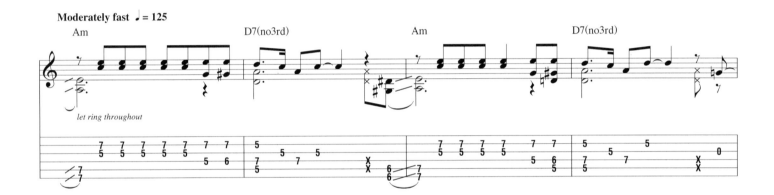

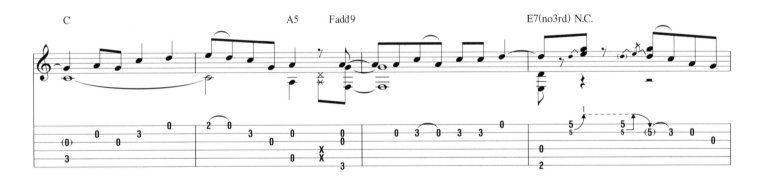

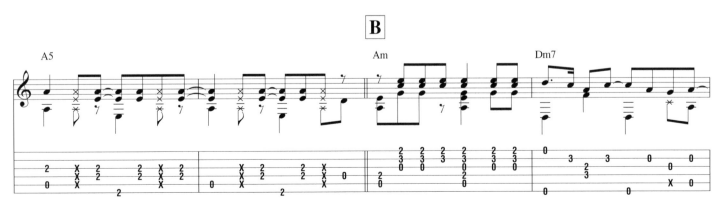

D

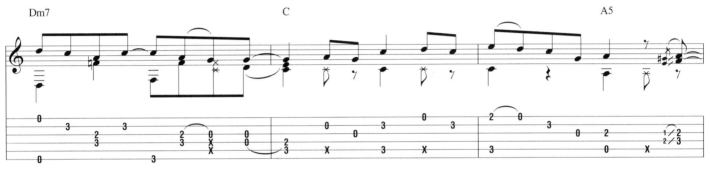

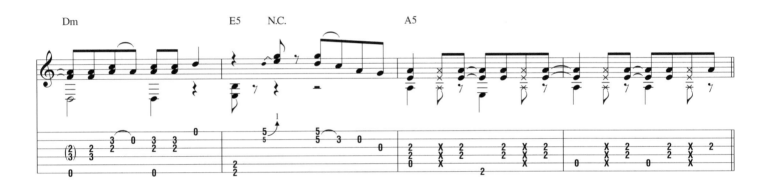

E

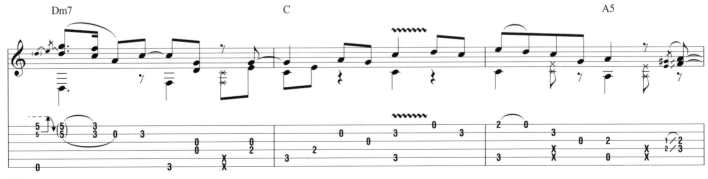

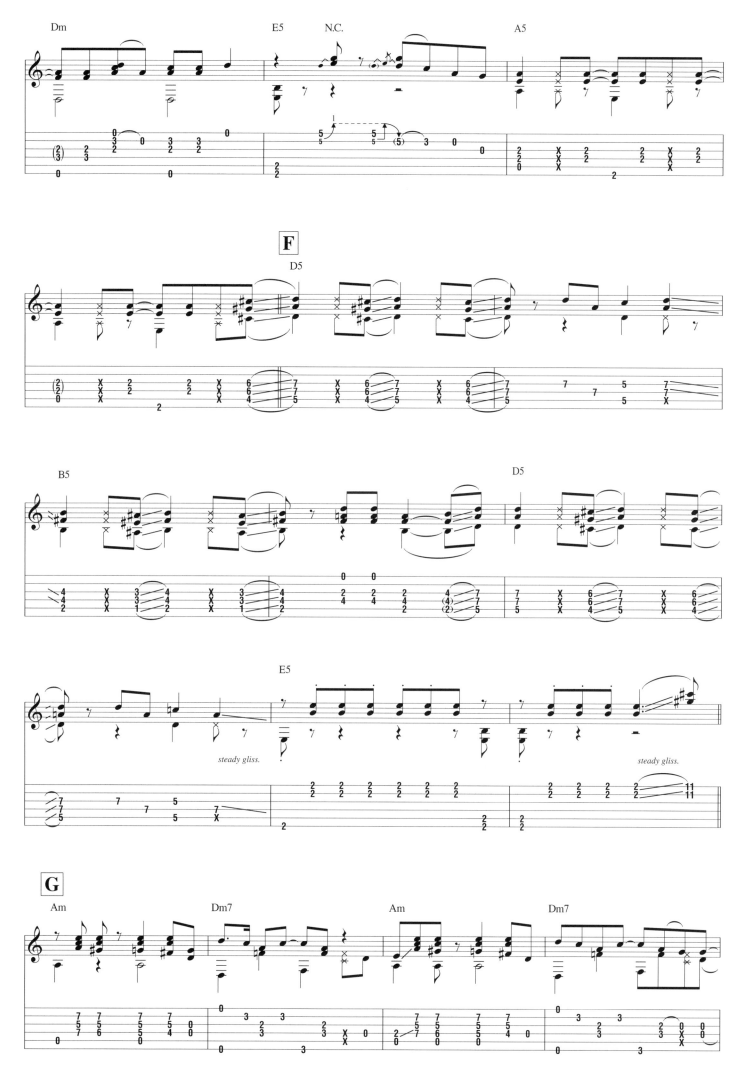

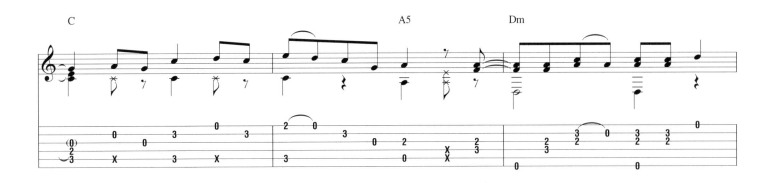

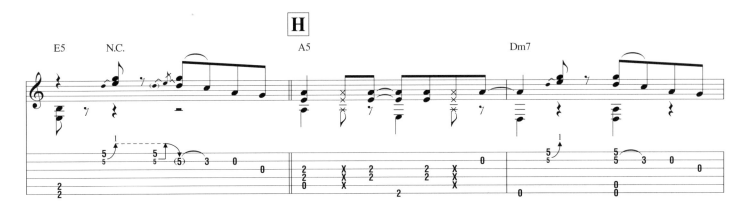

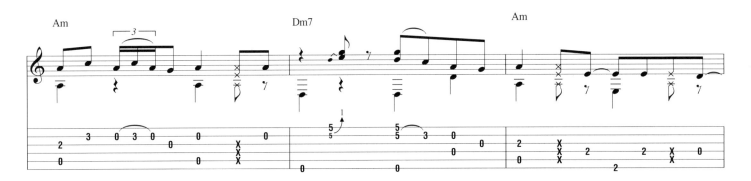

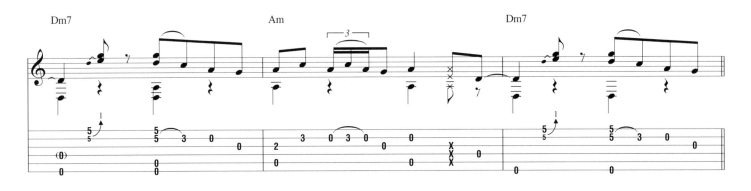

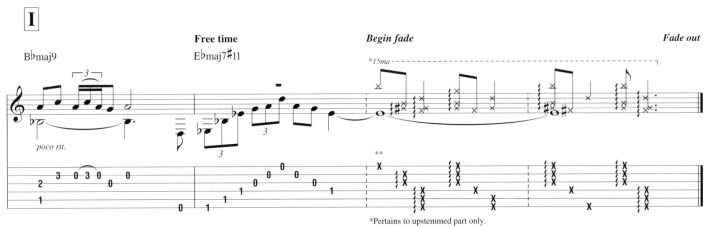

*Pertains to upstemmed part only.

**Pluck strings behind nut.

Ruby Baby

Words and Music by Jerry Leiber and Mike Stoller
Arranged by Wayne Johnson

Gtr. 2: Open G tuning:
(low to high) D-G-D-G-B-D

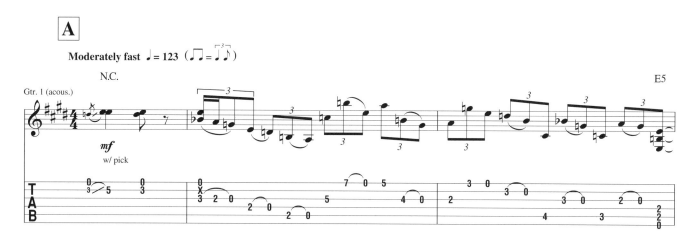

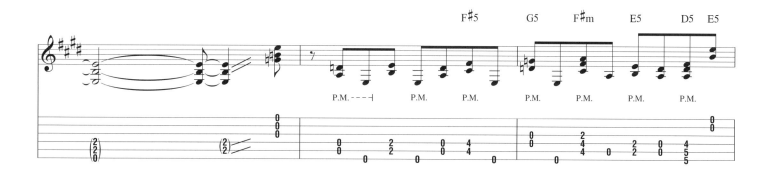

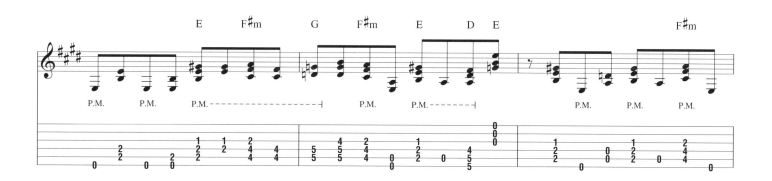

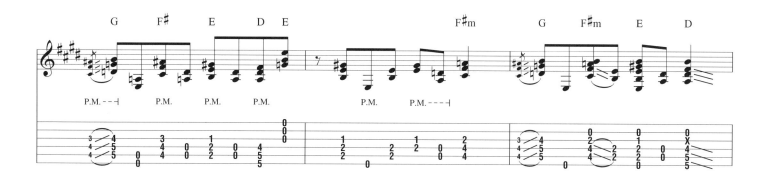

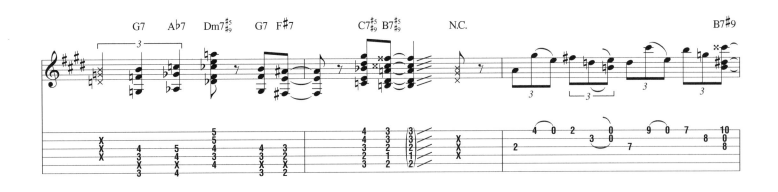

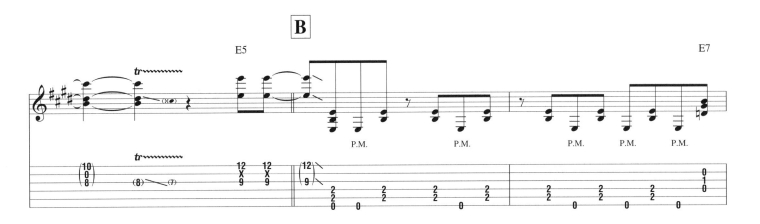

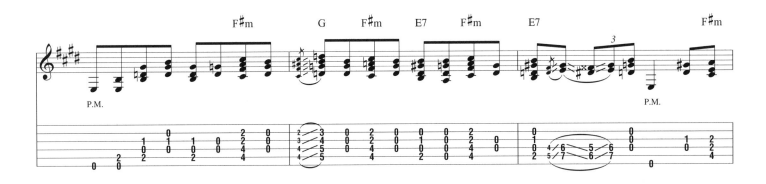

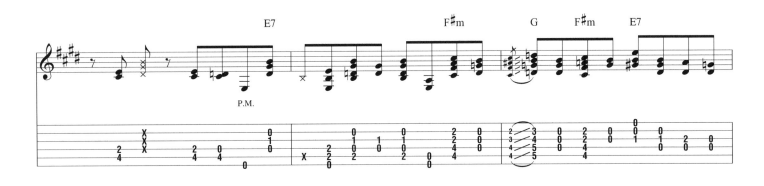

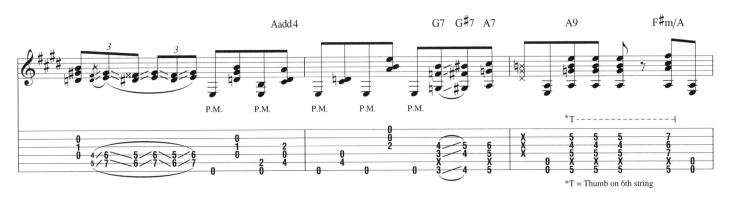

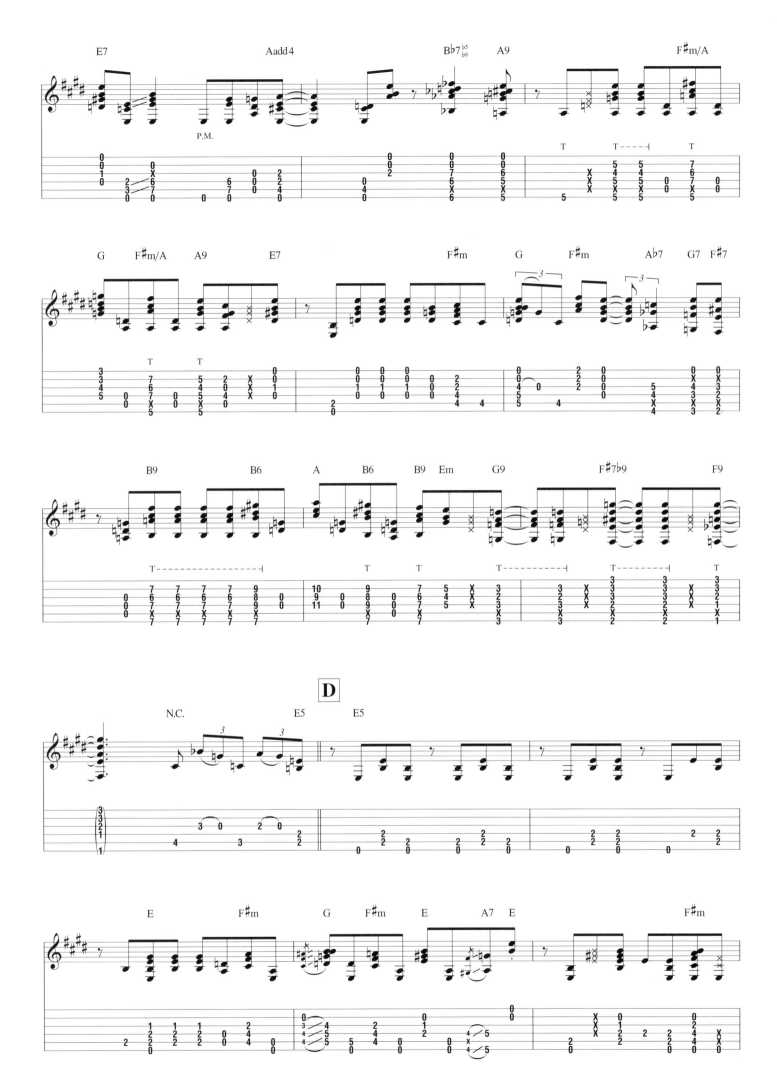

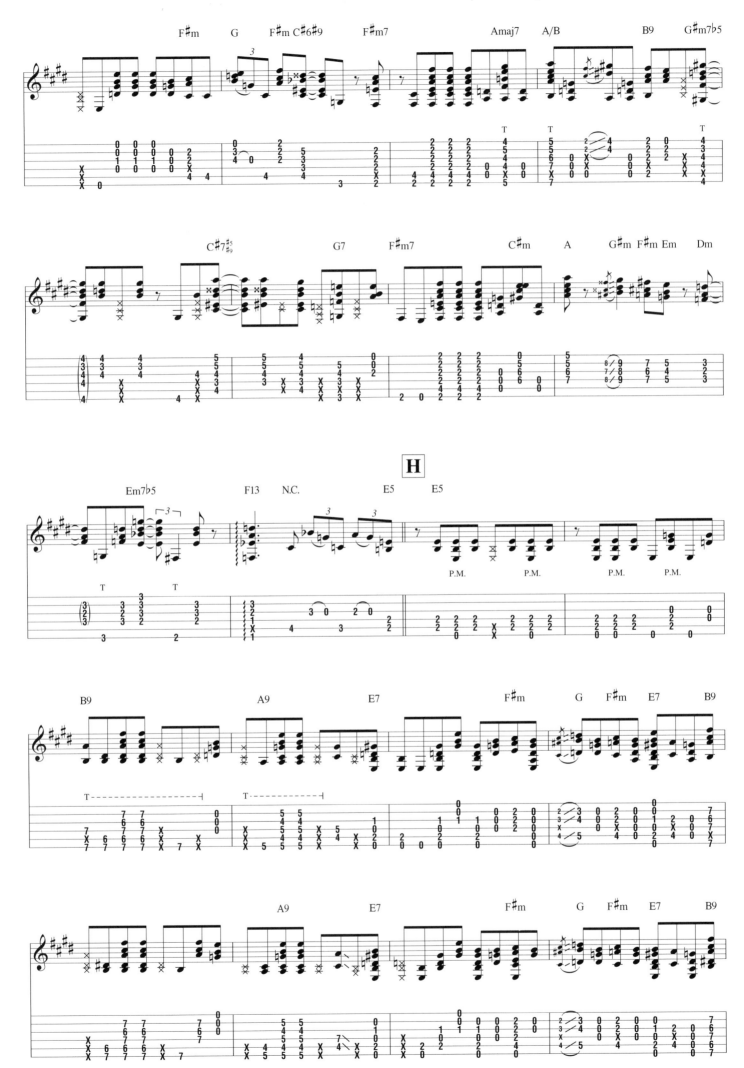

Hound Dog

Words and Music by Jerry Leiber and Mike Stoller
Arranged by Kenny Sultan

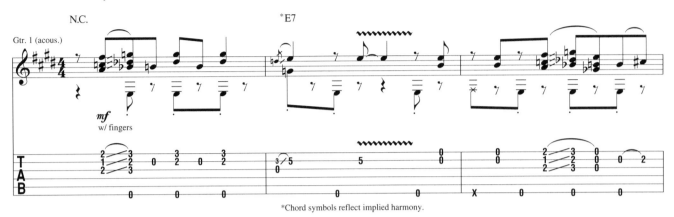

*Chord symbols reflect implied harmony.

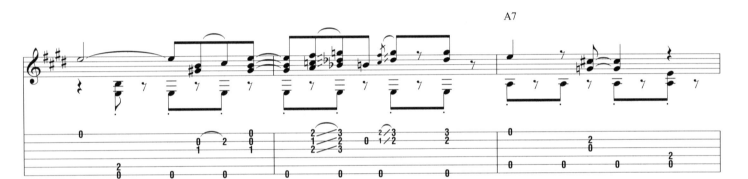

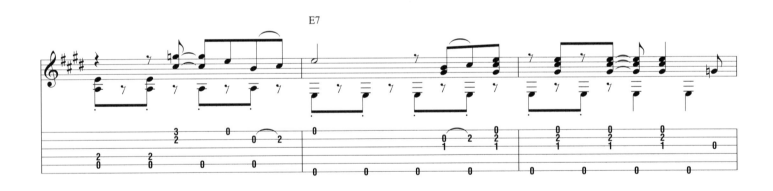

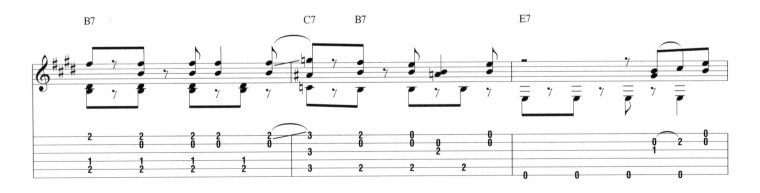

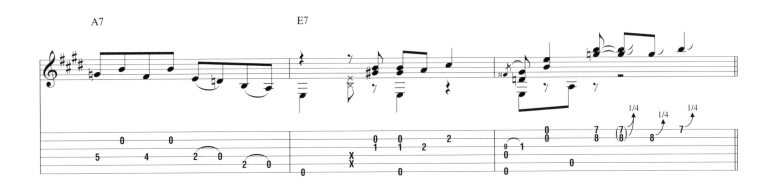

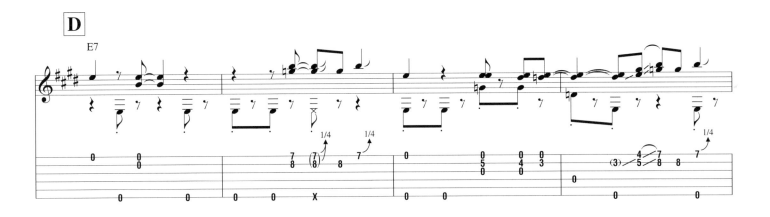

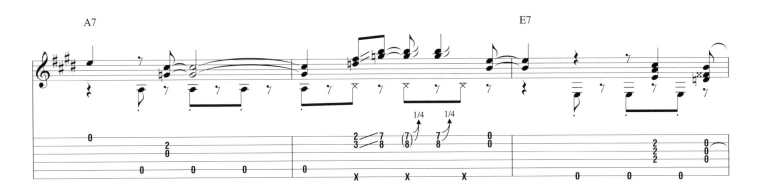

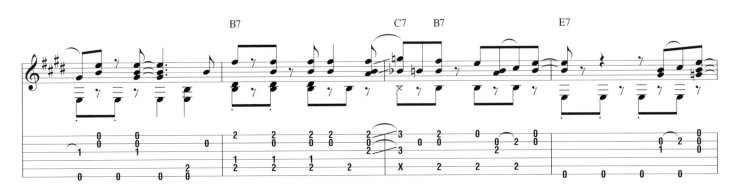

Yakety Yak

Words and Music by Jerry Leiber and Mike Stoller
Arranged by Doug Smith & Mark Hanson

*Chord symbols reflect implied harmony.

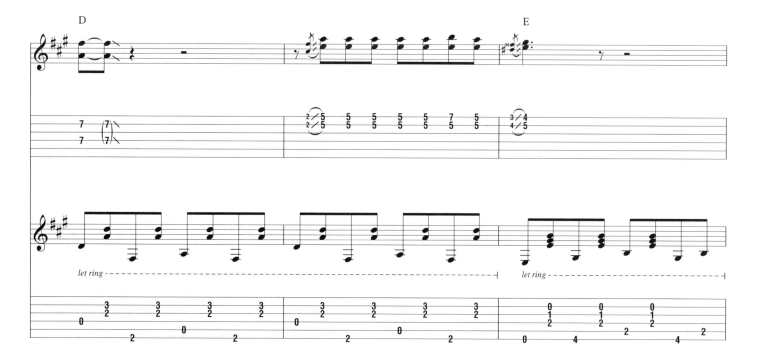

*K = Knock on soundboard w/ pick-hand middle finger.

w/ thumb pick & fingers

w/ fingers

*K = Knock on soundboard w/ pick-hand ring (a), middle (m), index (i) fingers & thumb (p).

**Tamburo: knock on bridge w/ pick-hand thumb.

C

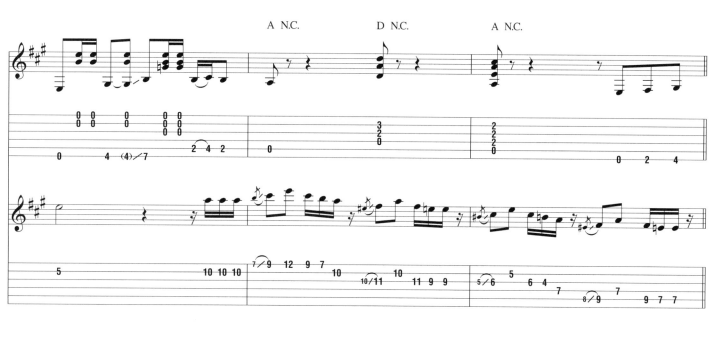

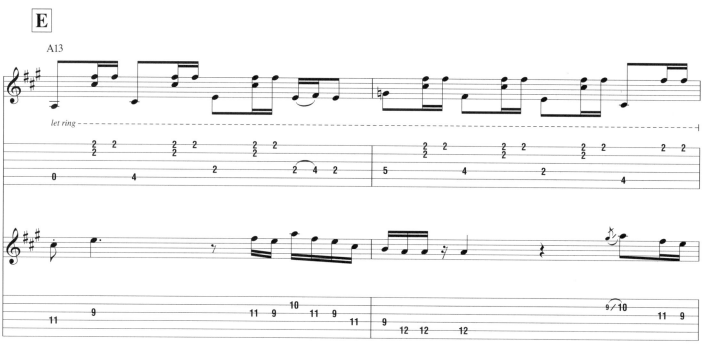

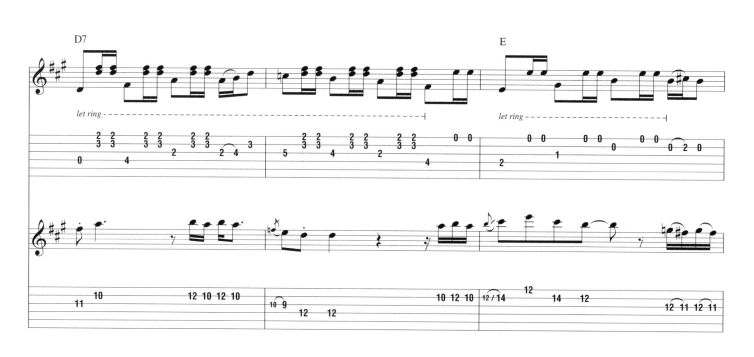

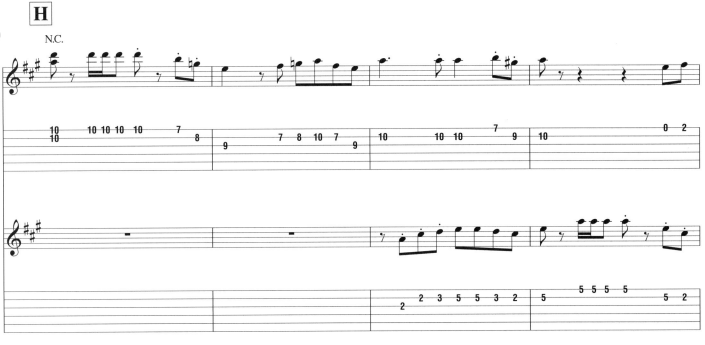

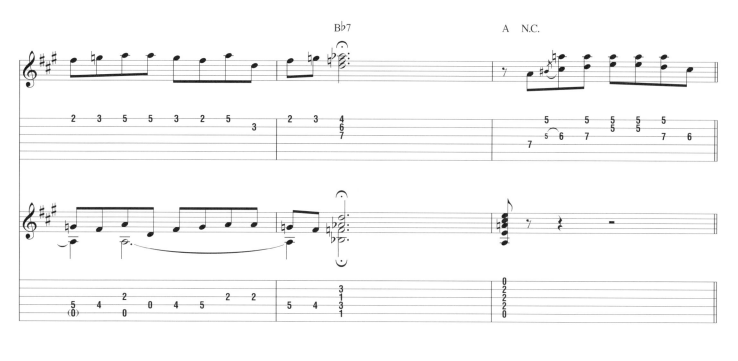

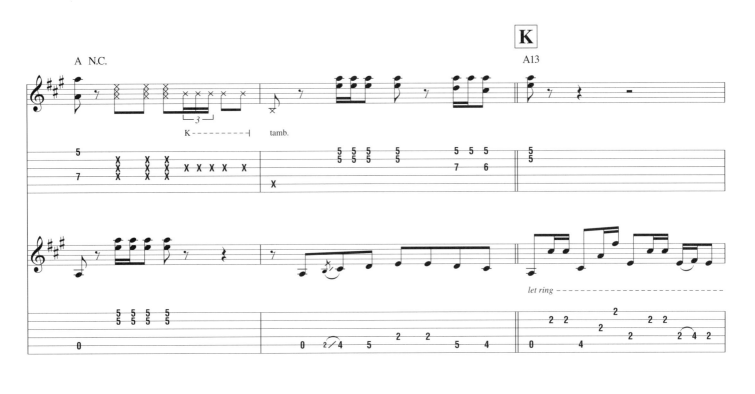

FINGERPICKING GUITAR BOOKS

Hone your fingerpicking skills with these great songbooks featuring solo guitar arrangements in standard notation and tablature. The arrangements in these books are carefully written for intermediate-level guitarists. Each song combines melody and harmony in one superb guitar fingerpicking arrangement. Each book also includes an introduction to basic fingerstyle guitar.

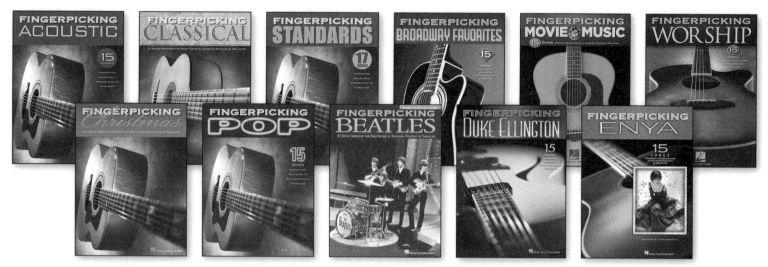

FINGERPICKING ACOUSTIC
00699614..$10.99

FINGERPICKING ACOUSTIC ROCK
00699764..$9.99

FINGERPICKING BACH
00699793..$8.95

FINGERPICKING BALLADS
00699717..$9.99

FINGERPICKING BEATLES
00699049..$19.99

FINGERPICKING BROADWAY FAVORITES
00699843..$9.99

FINGERPICKING BROADWAY HITS
00699838..$7.99

FINGERPICKING CELTIC FOLK
00701148..$7.99

FINGERPICKING CHILDREN'S SONGS
00699712..$9.99

FINGERPICKING CHRISTMAS
00699599..$8.95

FINGERPICKING CHRISTMAS CLASSICS
00701695..$7.99

FINGERPICKING CLASSICAL
00699620..$8.95

FINGERPICKING COUNTRY
00699687..$9.99

FINGERPICKING DISNEY
00699711..$10.99

FINGERPICKING DUKE ELLINGTON
00699845..$9.99

FINGERPICKING ENYA
00701161..$9.99

FINGERPICKING GOSPEL
00701059..$7.99

FINGERPICKING HYMNS
00699688..$8.95

FINGERPICKING IRISH SONGS
00701965..$7.99

FINGERPICKING JAZZ STANDARDS
00699840..$7.99

FINGERPICKING LATIN STANDARDS
00699837..$7.99

FINGERPICKING ANDREW LLOYD WEBBER
00699839..$9.99

FINGERPICKING LOVE SONGS
00699841..$7.99

FINGERPICKING LULLABYES
00701276..$9.99

FINGERPICKING MOVIE MUSIC
00699919..$9.99

FINGERPICKING MOZART
00699794..$8.95

FINGERPICKING POP
00699615..$9.99

FINGERPICKING PRAISE
00699714..$8.95

FINGERPICKING ROCK
00699716..$9.99

FINGERPICKING STANDARDS
00699613..$9.99

FINGERPICKING WEDDING
00699637..$9.99

FINGERPICKING WORSHIP
00700554..$7.99

FINGERPICKING NEIL YOUNG – GREATEST HITS
00700134..$12.99

FINGERPICKING YULETIDE
00699654..$9.99

HAL•LEONARD® CORPORATION
7777 W. BLUEMOUND RD. P.O. BOX 13819 MILWAUKEE, WI 53213
Visit Hal Leonard online at www.halleonard.com

Prices, contents and availability subject to change without notice.

0312

RECORDED VERSIONS®

The Best Note-For-Note Transcriptions Available

RECORDED VERSIONS GUITAR®

ALL BOOKS INCLUDE TABLATURE

14037551 AC/DC – Backtracks $32.99
00692015 Aerosmith – Greatest Hits $22.95
00690178 Alice in Chains – Acoustic $19.95
00694865 Alice in Chains – Dirt $19.95
00690812 All American Rejects – Move Along $19.95
00690958 Duane Allman Guitar Anthology $24.99
00694932 Allman Brothers Band – Volume 1 .... $24.95
00694933 Allman Brothers Band – Volume 2 .... $24.95
00694934 Allman Brothers Band – Volume 3 .... $24.95
00690865 Atreyu – A Deathgrip on Yesterday $19.95
00690609 Audioslave $19.95
00690820 Avenged Sevenfold – City of Evil $24.95
00691065 Avenged Sevenfold – Waking the Fallen $22.99
00690503 Beach Boys – Very Best of $19.95
00690489 Beatles – 1 .... $24.99
00694832 Beatles – For Acoustic Guitar $22.99
00691014 Beatles Rock Band $34.99
00690110 Beatles – White Album (Book 1) $19.95
00691043 Jeff Beck – Wired $19.99
00692385 Chuck Berry $19.95
00690835 Billy Talent $19.95
00690901 Best of Black Sabbath $19.95
00690831 blink-182 – Greatest Hits $19.95
00690913 Boston $19.95
00690932 Boston – Don't Look Back $19.99
00690491 David Bowie – Best of $19.95
00690873 Breaking Benjamin – Phobia $19.95
00690451 Jeff Buckley – Collection $24.95
00690957 Bullet for My Valentine – Scream Aim Fire $22.99
00691004 Chickenfoot $22.99
00690590 Eric Clapton – Anthology $29.95
00690415 Clapton Chronicles – Best of Eric Clapton $18.95
00690936 Eric Clapton – Complete Clapton $29.99
00690074 Eric Clapton – The Cream of Clapton $24.95
00694869 Eric Clapton – Unplugged $22.95
00690162 The Clash – Best of $19.95
00690828 Coheed & Cambria – Good Apollo I'm Burning Star, IV, Vol. 1: From Fear Through the Eyes of Madness $19.95
00690593 Coldplay – A Rush of Blood to the Head $19.95
00690962 Coldplay – Viva La Vida $19.95
00690819 Creedence Clearwater Revival – Best of $22.95
00690648 The Very Best of Jim Croce $19.95
00690613 Crosby, Stills & Nash – Best of $22.95
00690967 Death Cab for Cutie – Narrow Stairs $22.99
00690289 Deep Purple – Best of $19.99
00690784 Def Leppard – Best of $19.95
00692240 Bo Diddley $19.99
00690347 The Doors – Anthology $22.95
00690348 The Doors – Essential Guitar Collection $16.95
00690810 Fall Out Boy – From Under the Cork Tree $19.95
00691181 Five Finger Death Punch – American Capitalist $22.99
00690664 Fleetwood Mac – Best of $19.95
00690870 Flyleaf $19.95
00690931 Foo Fighters – Echoes, Silence, Patience & Grace $19.95
00690808 Foo Fighters – In Your Honor $19.95
00691115 Foo Fighters – Wasting Light $22.99
00690805 Robben Ford – Best of $22.99
00694920 Free – Best of $19.95
00691050 Glee Guitar Collection $19.99
00690943 The Goo Goo Dolls – Greatest Hits Volume 1: The Singles $22.95
00701764 Guitar Tab White Pages – Play-Along $39.99
00694854 Buddy Guy – Damn Right, I've Got the Blues $19.95

00690840 Ben Harper – Both Sides of the Gun $19.95
00694798 George Harrison – Anthology $19.95
00690841 Scott Henderson – Blues Guitar Collection $19.95
00692930 Jimi Hendrix – Are You Experienced? $24.95
00692931 Jimi Hendrix – Axis: Bold As Love $22.95
00692932 Jimi Hendrix – Electric Ladyland $24.95
00690017 Jimi Hendrix – Live at Woodstock $24.95
00690602 Jimi Hendrix – Smash Hits $24.99
00690793 John Lee Hooker Anthology $24.99
00690692 Billy Idol – Very Best of $19.95
00690688 Incubus – A Crow Left of the Murder $19.95
00690544 Incubus – Morningview $19.95
00690790 Iron Maiden Anthology $24.99
00690721 Jet – Get Born $19.95
00690684 Jethro Tull – Aqualung $19.95
00690959 John5 – Requiem $22.95
00690814 John5 – Songs for Sanity $19.95
00690751 John5 – Vertigo $19.95
00690845 Eric Johnson – Bloom $19.95
00690846 Jack Johnson and Friends – Sing-A-Longs and Lullabies for the Film Curious George $19.95
00690271 Robert Johnson – New Transcriptions $24.95
00699131 Janis Joplin – Best of $19.95
00690427 Judas Priest – Best of $22.99
00690975 Kings of Leon – Only by the Night $22.99
00694903 Kiss – Best of $24.95
00690355 Kiss – Destroyer $16.95
00690834 Lamb of God – Ashes of the Wake $19.95
00690875 Lamb of God – Sacrament $19.95
00690823 Ray LaMontagne – Trouble $19.95
00690679 John Lennon – Guitar Collection $19.95
00690781 Linkin Park – Hybrid Theory $22.95
00690743 Los Lonely Boys $19.95
00690720 Lostprophets – Start Something $19.95
00690955 Lynyrd Skynyrd – All-Time Greatest Hits $19.99
00694954 Lynyrd Skynyrd – New Best of $19.95
00690754 Marilyn Manson – Lest We Forget $19.95
00694956 Bob Marley– Legend $19.95
00694945 Bob Marley– Songs of Freedom $24.95
00690657 Maroon5 – Songs About Jane $19.95
00120080 Don McLean – Songbook $19.95
00694951 Megadeth – Rust in Peace $22.95
00690951 Megadeth – United Abominations $22.99
00690505 John Mellencamp – Guitar Collection $19.95
00690646 Pat Metheny – One Quiet Night $19.95
00690558 Pat Metheny – Trio: 99>00 .... $19.95
00690040 Steve Miller Band – Young Hearts $19.95
00691070 Mumford & Sons – Sigh No More $22.99
00694883 Nirvana – Nevermind $19.95
00690026 Nirvana – Unplugged in New York $19.95
00690807 The Offspring – Greatest Hits $19.95
00694847 Ozzy Osbourne – Best of $22.95
00690399 Ozzy Osbourne – Ozzman Cometh $22.99
00690933 Best of Brad Paisley $22.95
00690995 Brad Paisley – Play: The Guitar Album $24.99
00690866 Panic! At the Disco – A Fever You Can't Sweat Out $19.95
00690938 Christopher Parkening – Duets & Concertos $24.99
00694855 Pearl Jam – Ten $19.95
00690439 A Perfect Circle – Mer De Noms $19.95
00690499 Tom Petty – Definitive Guitar Collection $19.95
00690428 Pink Floyd – Dark Side of the Moon $19.95
00690789 Poison – Best of $19.95
00693864 The Police – Best of $19.95
00694975 Queen – Greatest Hits $24.95
00690670 Queensryche – Very Best of $19.95

00690878 The Raconteurs – Broken Boy Soldiers $19.95
00694910 Rage Against the Machine $19.95
00690055 Red Hot Chili Peppers – Blood Sugar Sex Magik $19.95
00690584 Red Hot Chili Peppers – By the Way $19.95
00691166 Red Hot Chili Peppers – I'm with You $22.99
00690852 Red Hot Chili Peppers –Stadium Arcadium $24.95
00690511 Django Reinhardt – Definitive Collection $19.95
00690779 Relient K – MMHMM $19.95
00690631 Rolling Stones – Guitar Anthology $27.95
00694976 Rolling Stones – Some Girls $22.95
00690264 The Rolling Stones – Tattoo You $19.95
00690685 David Lee Roth – Eat 'Em and Smile $19.95
00690942 David Lee Roth and the Songs of Van Halen $19.95
00690031 Santana's Greatest Hits $19.95
00690566 Scorpions – Best of $22.95
00690604 Bob Seger – Guitar Collection $19.95
00690803 Kenny Wayne Shepherd Band – Best of $19.95
00690968 Shinedown – The Sound of Madness $22.99
00690813 Slayer – Guitar Collection $19.95
00690733 Slipknot – Vol. 3 (The Subliminal Verses) $22.99
00120004 Steely Dan – Best of $24.95
00694921 Steppenwolf – Best of $22.95
00690655 Mike Stern – Best of $19.95
00690877 Stone Sour – Come What(ever) May $19.95
00690520 Styx Guitar Collection $19.95
00120081 Sublime $19.95
00120122 Sublime – 40oz. to Freedom $19.95
00690929 Sum 41 – Underclass Hero $19.95
00690767 Switchfoot – The Beautiful Letdown $19.95
00690993 Taylor Swift – Fearless $22.99
00690830 System of a Down – Hypnotize $19.95
00690531 System of a Down – Toxicity $19.95
00694824 James Taylor – Best of $16.95
00690871 Three Days Grace – One-X $19.95
00690683 Robin Trower – Bridge of Sighs $19.95
00699191 U2 – Best of: 1980-1990 .... $19.95
00690732 U2 – Best of: 1990-2000 .... $19.95
00660137 Steve Vai – Passion & Warfare $24.95
00690116 Stevie Ray Vaughan – Guitar Collection $24.95
00660058 Stevie Ray Vaughan – Lightnin' Blues 1983-1987 .... $24.95
00694835 Stevie Ray Vaughan – The Sky Is Crying $22.95
00690015 Stevie Ray Vaughan – Texas Flood $19.95
00690772 Velvet Revolver – Contraband $22.95
00690071 Weezer (The Blue Album) $19.95
00690966 Weezer – (Red Album) $19.99
00690447 The Who – Best of $24.95
00690916 The Best of Dwight Yoakam $19.95
00690905 Neil Young – Rust Never Sleeps $19.99
00690623 Frank Zappa – Over-Nite Sensation $22.99
00690589 ZZ Top Guitar Anthology $24.95

FOR A COMPLETE LIST OF GUITAR RECORDED VERSIONS TITLES, SEE YOUR LOCAL MUSIC DEALER, OR WRITE TO:

HAL•LEONARD® CORPORATION

7777 W. BLUEMOUND RD. P.O. BOX 13819 MILWAUKEE, WI 53213

Visit Hal Leonard online at **www.halleonard.com**

Prices and availability subject to change without notice. Some products may not be available outside the U.S.A.

0212

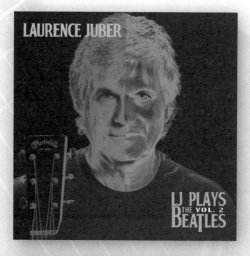
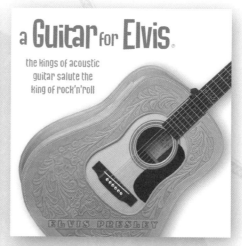
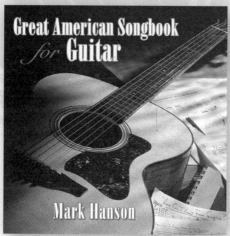
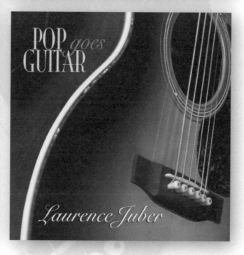
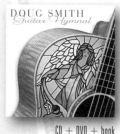